CH

# SILENTÓ
## BREAKOUT RAPPER

BY ALISHA GABRIEL

Published by The Child's World®
1980 Lookout Drive • Mankato, MN 56003-1705
800-599-READ • www.childsworld.com

ISBN 9781503819986
LCCN 2016960922

Printed in the United States of America
PA02335

ABOUT THE AUTHOR

Alisha Gabriel has a bachelor's degree and a master's degree in music
education from Texas State University. She lives near Austin, Texas. This is
her first book for children.

# TABLE OF
# CONTENTS

FAST FACTS.................................... 4

## Chapter 1
FIRST STEPS IN MUSIC ................. 7

## Chapter 2
TAKING ACTION........................... 11

## Chapter 3
SHARING THE SPOTLIGHT............ 15

## Chapter 4
NEXT STEPS ................................. 19

Think About It  21
Glossary  22
Source Notes  23
To Learn More  24
Index  24

# FAST FACTS

## Name

- Ricky Lamar Hawk, also known as Silentó

## Birthdate

- January 22, 1998

## Birthplace

- Atlanta, Georgia

## Fun Trivia

- Ricky chose the name Silentó because, to him, it means "less talk, more action."[1]
- Some of Ricky's musical role models are Usher, Mariah Carey, Ciara, and Future.
- Ricky would love to collaborate with Dr. Dre.
- Ricky never took dance lessons, but he wants to learn more moves.
- Ricky **performed** at the White House in Washington, DC, before the 2016 Easter Egg Roll.

# FIRST STEPS IN MUSIC

One afternoon during his junior year of high school, Ricky Hawk sat in the cafeteria with his friends. He thought up a catchy phrase and started rapping it. People at other tables turned around to watch him, so he called the song "Watch Me." What would happen if he switched the words around? He tried it about five different ways. His friends liked it and told him to record it. Out in the hallway, Ricky held up his phone and stared into the camera. Someone tapped a beat on a desk. Ricky made a 15-second video using the words, "Watch me Nae Nae, now watch me Whip." Later, he would switch the words around again. With the touch of a button, he posted it on a social media sharing site.

◀ **Ricky Hawk, also known as Silentó, has always liked to perform.**

Within a day, his video received hundreds of comments. He knew it would be a hit.

Even as a child, music was a part of Ricky's life. Growing up, Ricky used to sit with his mother in their living room and listen to Marvin Gaye and the Temptations. He also liked hanging out with friends from his apartment building. Ricky and his friends spent a lot of time listening to popular music on television and practicing new dance moves.

Things changed in eighth grade when Ricky did more than listen. He started doing his own rapping, singing, and dancing. Ricky and some friends started their own music group, called Young Swagg Kids, or YSK. The group didn't last long. But Ricky still wanted to make music, and he wanted the world to hear.

**Ricky has been into dancing and many kinds ▶ of music since he was very young.**

## Chapter 2

# TAKING ACTION

Ricky traveled to Temple **Studios** in Atlanta, Georgia, to work with his **producer**. Only a splash of color dressed up the outside of the white building. Inside, there were rooms with computers and gear for recording music.

Ricky wanted a career in the music business. That's why he worked with a producer. It was hard work writing music and finding places to **perform**. "I used to have to pay to perform at places, like skating rinks and teen parties," said Ricky. "I had to pay *them* to perform."[2] Some people thought Ricky was wasting his time and money. They said he wouldn't make it in the music business. Even Ricky's sister told him he wouldn't make it on the radio. Those comments only made him work harder.

◄ **Many people work together to make hip-hop songs. Ricky sings or raps while his DJ plays music or beats.**

This time, when Ricky walked into the studio, he had a plan. He couldn't wait to tell his producer about all the comments he had received for "Watch Me." That 15-second video was a hit. The words of the song ran through his head. Ricky could think of nothing else.

When Ricky saw his producer, he smiled, showing his dimples. He told his producer about "Watch Me" and asked if he could record the song. His producer said no. Not giving up, Ricky asked again. His producer told him to forget it. But Ricky couldn't forget about the song. In December 2014, his producer agreed to record the song, just to make Ricky happy. The words had changed a little from the first 15-second video, but these felt right. With the touch of a button, Ricky posted it online.

"I just want people to have fun. It's like people start smiling and all the bad goes away when my song comes on. It's rated E for everyone!"[3]

—Silentó

**Ricky's dimples are part of his charm.** ▶

## Chapter 3

# SHARING THE SPOTLIGHT

In May 2015, Ricky sat facing the camera with a computer and speakers behind him. He talked to his fans, who knew him as Silentó. "I've been seeing you all trying to do my dance, but let me really show you how it's done. Watch me." Standing in front of a black brick wall, Ricky made a **tutorial**, showing all the dance moves to "Watch Me." People all over the world watched his video and learned the moves.

Ricky wasn't done. He wanted to make an official video with his fans, so he teamed up with the company DanceOn. Thousands of people posted their own dance videos with a special **hashtag**, #WatchMeDanceOn.

◀ **Ricky shows off his dance moves with DJ Grand on the red carpet at the MTV Video Music Awards in 2015.**

Some of those videos were watched millions of times! The DanceOn team chose their favorite fan videos to include in the official video.

Ricky said, "I wanted to bring my video more to the people, just like how I started it, by posting other people dancing to my song. I wanted people to have their clips of their song in my video."[4]

A month later, the official "Watch Me" video came out. It opened with five girls standing in a V-shape in front of a huge mural in Harlem, New York. Two more groups appeared on the screen, then another. Seconds later, the screen broke into six, 12, and then 48 small groups. Then tiny pictures formed the name Silentó, and "Watch Me" flashed onto the screen.

"I felt so honored to be in his music video. It was fun, because in my video, I got to add my own style, and it's a fun song for kids and adults to dance to."[5]

—Aidan Prince, a ten-year-old dancer in the official video

▲ **Ricky performs "Watch Me" with the cast of the television show *Black-ish* at the 2015 BET Awards.**

The camera cut to Ricky bouncing a basketball with colorful streamers above him and dancers behind him. Fans joined him as he performed "Watch Me."

# NEXT STEPS

Ricky sat down in a radio station studio. He put on headphones and pulled a microphone close to his mouth. Instead of his rapping or singing, people wanted to hear his story. They wanted to know how he wrote a song, recorded it, and made it famous while he was still in high school. "Watch Me" gained everyone's attention, including record companies. Ricky signed a contract with Capitol Records even before his official video came out.

"I want to make music for people to hear as a family," said Ricky. "But, I'm also the urban kid from Atlanta and I feel like there isn't anyone else like me. I'm real and I care about my fans."[6]

◄ **Ricky wants everyone to enjoy his music.**

▲ Ricky hopes "Watch Me" is just the start of a long career in the music business.

Ricky said he knew he had made it big when he performed "Watch Me" on *Good Morning America* in June 2015. The next summer, he joined the Let's Dance tour, performing all over the United States.

The tour kept him busy. But he still found time to work with other **musicians**. He teamed up with Punch to record "Spotlight," and he worked with 13-year-old Sophia Grace Brownlee on "Girl in the Mirror."

Many people have asked Silentó what he plans to do next. In addition to making music, he said, "I want to go to college. I want to get an education. I want to be prepared. . . . I want to make great songs for people that spread love. That's all I want, love."[7]

## THINK ABOUT IT

- Ricky had to convince his producer to let him record "Watch Me." How could other people's opinions affect your career path?
- Ricky found his first fans when he uploaded a video to his social media account. How has social media changed what or who becomes famous?
- What are the advantages or disadvantages of posting your work on the Internet?

# GLOSSARY

**hashtag (HASH-tag):** A hashtag is a symbol that looks like a pound sign. Words or phrases are typed after a hashtag to help people search for information about a topic. The hashtag #WatchMeDanceOn was used by Ricky to help people find videos for his song "Watch Me."

**musicians (mew-ZISH-uhns):** Musicians are people who make music by singing or playing instruments. Ricky sometimes works with other musicians to record songs.

**performed (pur-FORMD):** Someone who performed has sang, acted, or danced in front of others. Ricky has performed in front of large crowds.

**producer (pruh-DOO-suhr):** A producer makes the major decisions for projects such as plays, television shows, and movies. A music producer adds the beats and other instrument parts to songs. Ricky's producer finally let him record "Watch Me" in the studio.

**social media (SO-shul MEE-dee-uh):** Social media is a term used for websites and apps that allow large groups of people to share things with others. Ricky used social media to share his music with people long before he had a record deal.

**studios (STU-dee-ohs):** Studios are rooms or buildings made for a special purpose. The music studios where Ricky records music have all the gear needed to record a song.

**tutorial (too-TOR-ee-uhl):** When a teacher shows a small group of students how to do something, it is a tutorial. Ricky made a tutorial to show people how to dance to "Watch Me."

# SOURCE NOTES

1. Melissa Ruggieri. "Atlanta Rapper Silento Whips Fans into a YouTube Frenzy with 'Watch Me.'" *Atlanta Journal-Constitution*. Cox Media Group, 29 June 2015. Web. 7 Feb. 2017.

2. Ibid.

3. "Silento: 'Less Talk, More Action.'" *BlackDoctor*. BlackDoctor, 22 Jan. 2016. Web. 7 Feb. 2017.

4. "Inside The Silento — Watch Me (Whip/Nae Nae) Phenomenon: The Edge." *YouTube*. YouTube, 25 Apr. 2015. Web. 7 Feb. 2017.

5. Ibid.

6. Juan Ant. Bisono. "Silentó Made the World Whip and Nae Nae, and He Says He's Just Getting Started." *Miami New Times*. Miami New Times, 2 Apr. 2016. Web. 7 Feb. 2017.

7. Ibid.

8. "Inside The Silento — Watch Me (Whip/Nae Nae) Phenomenon: The Edge." *YouTube*. YouTube, 25 Apr. 2015. Web. 7 Feb. 2017.

# TO LEARN MORE

## Books

Giovanni, Nikki. *Hip Hop Speaks to Children: A Celebration of Poetry with a Beat*. Naperville, IL: Sourcebooks Jabberwocky, 2008.

Hill, Laban Carrick. *When the Beat Was Born: DJ Kool Herc and the Creation of Hip Hop*. New York, NY: Roaring Brook Press, 2013.

MattyB and Travis Thrasher. *That's a Rap*. New York, NY: Gallery Books, 2016.

## Web Sites

Visit our Web site for links about Silentó:

childsworld.com/links

*Note to Parents, Teachers, and Librarians: We routinely verify our Web links to make sure they are safe and active sites. So encourage your readers to check them out!*

# INDEX

Atlanta, 11, 19

Brownlee, Sophia Grace, 21

Capitol Records, 19

DanceOn, 15, 16

Gaye, Marvin, 8
"Girl in the Mirror," 21
*Good Morning America*, 20

hashtag, 15
high school, 7, 19

Let's Dance tour, 20

producer, 11, 12
Punch (musician), 21

Silentó (stage name), 15, 16, 21
social media, 7
"Spotlight," 21
studio, 11, 12, 19

Temptations, 8

"Watch Me," 7, 12, 15, 16–17, 19, 20

Young Swagg Kids, 8